Gratitude

Gratitude allows us to discover the many blessings we have and distracts us from the misfortunes that we face. By filling out this journal, you will develop positive habits that will improve your life in different ways.

"Gratitude will shift you to a higher frequency, and you will attract much better things."
- Rhonda Byrne

Research has shown that being grateful physically changes our brains. It boosts our self-esteem, enhances empathy, makes us sleep better and unshackles us from toxic emotions.

But that's not all of it. Gratitude brings a peacefulness, a quiet joy, to our lives and makes us appreciate the people around us and the things we do.
Doesn't it sound much better than being unhappy about the things we don't have?

Most important of all though:
Have **FUN** with this book!
Fill this journal with splashy doodles and your own words.
This is about YOU and no one else.

THOUGHT OF THE WEEK

I am not perfect
but I am unique.

Date: _____ **M T W T F S S**

I'm thankful for...

1. _____

2. _____

3. _____

Today this person was kind to me:

I felt...

○ _____ ○ Content   ○ Sad
○ _____ ○ Inspired   ○ Anxious
○ Serene   ○ Cheerful   ○ Overwhelmed
○ Happy   ○ Hilarious   ○ Annoyed
○ Loving   ○ Balanced   ○ Disappointed
○ Kind   ○ Stressed   ○ Angry

Memory, thought or doodle of the day:

Date: _____   **M T W T F S S**

I'm thankful for...

1. _____

2. _____

3. _____

Today I saw this act of kindness:

I felt...

- ○ _____
- ○ _____
- ○ Serene
- ○ Happy
- ○ Loving
- ○ Kind

- ○ Content
- ○ Inspired
- ○ Cheerful
- ○ Hilarious
- ○ Balanced
- ○ Stressed

- ○ Sad
- ○ Anxious
- ○ Overwhelmed
- ○ Annoyed
- ○ Disappointed
- ○ Angry

Memory, thought or doodle of the day:

Date: _____   **M T W T F S S**

I'm thankful for...

1. _____

2. _____

3. _____

Today I learned...

I felt...

- ○ _____
- ○ _____
- ○ Serene
- ○ Happy
- ○ Loving
- ○ Kind

- ○ Content
- ○ Inspired
- ○ Cheerful
- ○ Hilarious
- ○ Balanced
- ○ Stressed

- ○ Sad
- ○ Anxious
- ○ Overwhelmed
- ○ Annoyed
- ○ Disappointed
- ○ Angry

Memory, thought or doodle of the day:

Date: _____ **M T W T F S S**

I'm thankful for...

1. _____

2. _____

3. _____

Today I smiled because...

I felt...

○ _____ ○ Content   ○ Sad
○ _____ ○ Inspired   ○ Anxious
○ Serene   ○ Cheerful   ○ Overwhelmed
○ Happy   ○ Hilarious   ○ Annoyed
○ Loving   ○ Balanced   ○ Disappointed
○ Kind   ○ Stressed   ○ Angry

Memory, thought or doodle of the day:

Date: _____   **M T W T F S S**

I'm thankful for...

1. _____

2. _____

3. _____

I am grateful for this person:

I felt...

- ○ _____
- ○ _____
- ○ Serene
- ○ Happy
- ○ Loving
- ○ Kind

- ○ Content
- ○ Inspired
- ○ Cheerful
- ○ Hilarious
- ○ Balanced
- ○ Stressed

- ○ Sad
- ○ Anxious
- ○ Overwhelmed
- ○ Annoyed
- ○ Disappointed
- ○ Angry

Memory, thought or doodle of the day:

Date: _____ **M T W T F S S**

I'm thankful for...

1. _____

2. _____

3. _____

Things I did well today:

I felt...

- ○ _____
- ○ _____
- ○ Serene
- ○ Happy
- ○ Loving
- ○ Kind

- ○ Content
- ○ Inspired
- ○ Cheerful
- ○ Hilarious
- ○ Balanced
- ○ Stressed

- ○ Sad
- ○ Anxious
- ○ Overwhelmed
- ○ Annoyed
- ○ Disappointed
- ○ Angry

Memory, thought or doodle of the day:

Date: _____ **M T W T F S S**

I'm thankful for...

1. _____

2. _____

3. _____

I am grateful for this food:

I felt...

○ _____   ○ Content   ○ Sad
○ _____   ○ Inspired   ○ Anxious
○ Serene   ○ Cheerful   ○ Overwhelmed
○ Happy   ○ Hilarious   ○ Annoyed
○ Loving   ○ Balanced   ○ Disappointed
○ Kind   ○ Stressed   ○ Angry

Memory, thought or doodle of the day:

THOUGHT OF THE WEEK

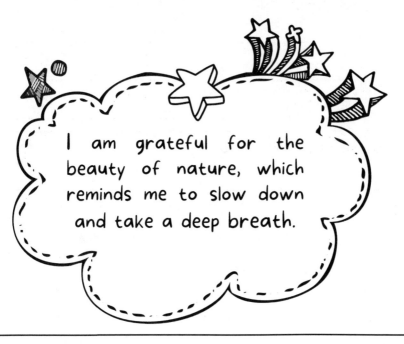

I am grateful for the beauty of nature, which reminds me to slow down and take a deep breath.

Write about an animal you are grateful for and explain why.

Date: _____   **M T W T F S S**

I'm thankful for...

1. _____

2. _____

3. _____

Today this person was kind to me:

I felt...

○ _____   ○ Content   ○ Sad
○ _____   ○ Inspired   ○ Anxious
○ Serene   ○ Cheerful   ○ Overwhelmed
○ Happy   ○ Hilarious   ○ Annoyed
○ Loving   ○ Balanced   ○ Disappointed
○ Kind   ○ Stressed   ○ Angry

Memory, thought or doodle of the day:

Date: _____ **M T W T F S S**

I'm thankful for...

1. _____

2. _____

3. _____

Today I saw this act of kindness:

I felt...

- ⭘ _____
- ⭘ _____
- ⭘ Serene
- ⭘ Happy
- ⭘ Loving
- ⭘ Kind

- ⭘ Content
- ⭘ Inspired
- ⭘ Cheerful
- ⭘ Hilarious
- ⭘ Balanced
- ⭘ Stressed

- ⭘ Sad
- ⭘ Anxious
- ⭘ Overwhelmed
- ⭘ Annoyed
- ⭘ Disappointed
- ⭘ Angry

Memory, thought or doodle of the day:

Date: _____   **M T W T F S S**

I'm thankful for...

1. _____

2. _____

3. _____

Today I learned...

I felt...

- ○ _____
- ○ _____
- ○ Serene
- ○ Happy
- ○ Loving
- ○ Kind

- ○ Content
- ○ Inspired
- ○ Cheerful
- ○ Hilarious
- ○ Balanced
- ○ Stressed

- ○ Sad
- ○ Anxious
- ○ Overwhelmed
- ○ Annoyed
- ○ Disappointed
- ○ Angry

Memory, thought or doodle of the day:

Date: _____ **M T W T F S S**

I'm thankful for...

1. _____

2. _____

3. _____

Today I smiled because...

I felt...

○ _____   ○ Content   ○ Sad

○ _____   ○ Inspired   ○ Anxious

○ Serene   ○ Cheerful   ○ Overwhelmed

○ Happy   ○ Hilarious   ○ Annoyed

○ Loving   ○ Balanced   ○ Disappointed

○ Kind   ○ Stressed   ○ Angry

Memory, thought or doodle of the day:

Date: _____ **M T W T F S S**

I'm thankful for...

1. _____

2. _____

3. _____

I am grateful for this person:

I felt...

○ _____   ○ Content   ○ Sad

○ _____   ○ Inspired   ○ Anxious

○ Serene   ○ Cheerful   ○ Overwhelmed

○ Happy   ○ Hilarious   ○ Annoyed

○ Loving   ○ Balanced   ○ Disappointed

○ Kind   ○ Stressed   ○ Angry

Memory, thought or doodle of the day:

Date: _____ **M T W T F S S**

I'm thankful for...

1. _____

2. _____

3. _____

Things I did well today:

I felt...

○ _____   ○ Content   ○ Sad
○ _____   ○ Inspired   ○ Anxious
○ Serene   ○ Cheerful   ○ Overwhelmed
○ Happy   ○ Hilarious   ○ Annoyed
○ Loving   ○ Balanced   ○ Disappointed
○ Kind   ○ Stressed   ○ Angry

Memory, thought or doodle of the day:

Date: _____ **M T W T F S S**

I'm thankful for...

1. _____

2. _____

3. _____

I am grateful for this food:

I felt...

○ _____ ○ Content ○ Sad
○ _____ ○ Inspired ○ Anxious
○ Serene ○ Cheerful ○ Overwhelmed
○ Happy ○ Hilarious ○ Annoyed
○ Loving ○ Balanced ○ Disappointed
○ Kind ○ Stressed ○ Angry

Memory, thought or doodle of the day:

THOUGHT OF THE WEEK

"We must find time to stop and thank the people who make a difference in our lives." - John F. Kennedy

Write about someone who inspires you.
Who do you look up to?

_____

_____

_____

_____

_____

_____

_____

_____

_____

Date: _____ **M T W T F S S**

I'm thankful for...

1. _____

2. _____

3. _____

Today this person was kind to me:

I felt...

- ○ _____
- ○ _____
- ○ Serene
- ○ Happy
- ○ Loving
- ○ Kind

- ○ Content
- ○ Inspired
- ○ Cheerful
- ○ Hilarious
- ○ Balanced
- ○ Stressed

- ○ Sad
- ○ Anxious
- ○ Overwhelmed
- ○ Annoyed
- ○ Disappointed
- ○ Angry

Memory, thought or doodle of the day:

Date: _____   **M T W T F S S**

I'm thankful for...

1. _____

2. _____

3. _____

Today I saw this act of kindness:

I felt...

○ _____   ○ Content   ○ Sad
○ _____   ○ Inspired   ○ Anxious
○ Serene   ○ Cheerful   ○ Overwhelmed
○ Happy   ○ Hilarious   ○ Annoyed
○ Loving   ○ Balanced   ○ Disappointed
○ Kind   ○ Stressed   ○ Angry

Memory, thought or doodle of the day:

Date: _____   **M T W T F S S**

I'm thankful for...

1. _____

2. _____

3. _____

Today I learned...

I felt...

○ _____   ○ Content   ○ Sad
○ _____   ○ Inspired   ○ Anxious
○ Serene   ○ Cheerful   ○ Overwhelmed
○ Happy   ○ Hilarious   ○ Annoyed
○ Loving   ○ Balanced   ○ Disappointed
○ Kind   ○ Stressed   ○ Angry

Memory, thought or doodle of the day:

Date: _____   **M T W T F S S**

I'm thankful for...

1. _____

2. _____

3. _____

Today I smiled because...

I felt...

○ _____   ○ Content   ○ Sad
○ _____   ○ Inspired   ○ Anxious
○ Serene   ○ Cheerful   ○ Overwhelmed
○ Happy   ○ Hilarious   ○ Annoyed
○ Loving   ○ Balanced   ○ Disappointed
○ Kind   ○ Stressed   ○ Angry

Memory, thought or doodle of the day:

Date: _____   **M T W T F S S**

I'm thankful for...

1. _____

2. _____

3. _____

I am grateful for this person:

I felt...

○ _____   ○ Content   ○ Sad
○ _____   ○ Inspired   ○ Anxious
○ Serene   ○ Cheerful   ○ Overwhelmed
○ Happy   ○ Hilarious ○ Annoyed
○ Loving   ○ Balanced   ○ Disappointed
○ Kind   ○ Stressed   ○ Angry

Memory, thought or doodle of the day:

Date: _____   **M T W T F S S**

I'm thankful for...

1. _____

2. _____

3. _____

Things I did well today:

I felt...

○ _____ ○ Content ○ Sad
○ _____ ○ Inspired ○ Anxious
○ Serene ○ Cheerful ○ Overwhelmed
○ Happy ○ Hilarious ○ Annoyed
○ Loving ○ Balanced ○ Disappointed
○ Kind ○ Stressed ○ Angry

Memory, thought or doodle of the day:

Date: _____ **M T W T F S S**

I'm thankful for...

1._____

2._____

3._____

I am grateful for this food:

I felt...

- ○ _____
- ○ _____
- ○ Serene
- ○ Happy
- ○ Loving
- ○ Kind

- ○ Content
- ○ Inspired
- ○ Cheerful
- ○ Hilarious
- ○ Balanced
- ○ Stressed

- ○ Sad
- ○ Anxious
- ○ Overwhelmed
- ○ Annoyed
- ○ Disappointed
- ○ Angry

Memory, thought or doodle of the day:

THOUGHT OF THE WEEK

"Plant seeds of happiness, hope, success, and love; it will all come back to you in abundance. This is the law of nature." - Steve Maraboli

How can you show that you're grateful?

Date: _____ **M T W T F S S**

I'm thankful for...

1. _____

2. _____

3. _____

Today this person was kind to me:

I felt...

○ _____ ○ Content   ○ Sad
○ _____ ○ Inspired   ○ Anxious
○ Serene   ○ Cheerful   ○ Overwhelmed
○ Happy   ○ Hilarious   ○ Annoyed
○ Loving   ○ Balanced   ○ Disappointed
○ Kind   ○ Stressed   ○ Angry

Memory, thought or doodle of the day:

Date: _____   **M T W T F S S**

I'm thankful for...

1. _____

2. _____

3. _____

Today I saw this act of kindness:

I felt...

- O _____
- O _____
- O Serene
- O Happy
- O Loving
- O Kind

- O Content
- O Inspired
- O Cheerful
- O Hilarious
- O Balanced
- O Stressed

- O Sad
- O Anxious
- O Overwhelmed
- O Annoyed
- O Disappointed
- O Angry

Memory, thought or doodle of the day:

Date: _____ **M T W T F S S**

I'm thankful for...

1. _____

2. _____

3. _____

Today I learned...

I felt...

○ _____ ○ Content ○ Sad

○ _____ ○ Inspired ○ Anxious

○ Serene ○ Cheerful ○ Overwhelmed

○ Happy ○ Hilarious ○ Annoyed

○ Loving ○ Balanced ○ Disappointed

○ Kind ○ Stressed ○ Angry

Memory, thought or doodle of the day:

Date: _____ **M T W T F S S**

I'm thankful for...

1. _____

2. _____

3. _____

Today I smiled because...

I felt...

○ _____   ○ Content   ○ Sad
○ _____   ○ Inspired   ○ Anxious
○ Serene   ○ Cheerful   ○ Overwhelmed
○ Happy   ○ Hilarious   ○ Annoyed
○ Loving   ○ Balanced   ○ Disappointed
○ Kind   ○ Stressed   ○ Angry

Memory, thought or doodle of the day:

Date: _____   **M T W T F S S**

I'm thankful for...

1. _____

2. _____

3. _____

I am grateful for this person:

I felt...

○ _____   ○ Content   ○ Sad
○ _____   ○ Inspired   ○ Anxious
○ Serene   ○ Cheerful   ○ Overwhelmed
○ Happy   ○ Hilarious   ○ Annoyed
○ Loving   ○ Balanced   ○ Disappointed
○ Kind   ○ Stressed   ○ Angry

Memory, thought or doodle of the day:

Date: _____   **M T W T F S S**

I'm thankful for...

1. _____

2. _____

3. _____

Things I did well today:

I felt...

○ _____   ○ Content   ○ Sad
○ _____   ○ Inspired   ○ Anxious
○ Serene   ○ Cheerful   ○ Overwhelmed
○ Happy   ○ Hilarious   ○ Annoyed
○ Loving   ○ Balanced   ○ Disappointed
○ Kind   ○ Stressed   ○ Angry

Memory, thought or doodle of the day:

Date: _____ **M T W T F S S**

I'm thankful for...

1. _____

2. _____

3. _____

I am grateful for this food:

I felt...

○ _____   ○ Content   ○ Sad

○ _____   ○ Inspired   ○ Anxious

○ Serene   ○ Cheerful   ○ Overwhelmed

○ Happy   ○ Hilarious   ○ Annoyed

○ Loving   ○ Balanced   ○ Disappointed

○ Kind   ○ Stressed   ○ Angry

Memory, thought or doodle of the day:

THOUGHT OF THE WEEK

"Happiness is not something ready-made. It comes from your own actions."
- Dalai Lama XIV

Things you'd like to do:

Date: _____ **M T W T F S S**

I'm thankful for...

1. _____

2. _____

3. _____

Today this person was kind to me:

I felt...

○ _____ ○ Content ○ Sad

○ _____ ○ Inspired ○ Anxious

○ Serene ○ Cheerful ○ Overwhelmed

○ Happy ○ Hilarious ○ Annoyed

○ Loving ○ Balanced ○ Disappointed

○ Kind ○ Stressed ○ Angry

Memory, thought or doodle of the day:

Date: _____   **M T W T F S S**

I'm thankful for...

1. _____

2. _____

3. _____

Today I saw this act of kindness:

I felt...

○ _____   ○ Content   ○ Sad
○ _____   ○ Inspired   ○ Anxious
○ Serene   ○ Cheerful   ○ Overwhelmed
○ Happy   ○ Hilarious   ○ Annoyed
○ Loving   ○ Balanced   ○ Disappointed
○ Kind   ○ Stressed   ○ Angry

Memory, thought or doodle of the day:

Date: _____ **M T W T F S S**

I'm thankful for...

1. _____

2. _____

3. _____

Today I learned...

I felt...

- ○ _____
- ○ _____
- ○ Serene
- ○ Happy
- ○ Loving
- ○ Kind

- ○ Content
- ○ Inspired
- ○ Cheerful
- ○ Hilarious
- ○ Balanced
- ○ Stressed

- ○ Sad
- ○ Anxious
- ○ Overwhelmed
- ○ Annoyed
- ○ Disappointed
- ○ Angry

Memory, thought or doodle of the day:

Date: _____   **M T W T F S S**

I'm thankful for...

1. _____

2. _____

3. _____

Today I smiled because...

I felt...

○ _____   ○ Content   ○ Sad

○ _____   ○ Inspired   ○ Anxious

○ Serene   ○ Cheerful   ○ Overwhelmed

○ Happy   ○ Hilarious   ○ Annoyed

○ Loving   ○ Balanced   ○ Disappointed

○ Kind   ○ Stressed   ○ Angry

Memory, thought or doodle of the day:

Date: _____   **M T W T F S S**

I'm thankful for...

1. _____

2. _____

3. _____

I am grateful for this person:

I felt...

○ _____	○ Content	○ Sad
○ _____	○ Inspired	○ Anxious
○ Serene	○ Cheerful	○ Overwhelmed
○ Happy	○ Hilarious	○ Annoyed
○ Loving	○ Balanced	○ Disappointed
○ Kind	○ Stressed	○ Angry

Memory, thought or doodle of the day:

Date: _____   **M T W T F S S**

I'm thankful for...

1. _____

2. _____

3. _____

Things I did well today:

I felt...

○ _____ ○ Content ○ Sad
○ _____ ○ Inspired ○ Anxious
○ Serene ○ Cheerful ○ Overwhelmed
○ Happy ○ Hilarious ○ Annoyed
○ Loving ○ Balanced ○ Disappointed
○ Kind ○ Stressed ○ Angry

Memory, thought or doodle of the day:

Date: _____   **M T W T F S S**

I'm thankful for...

1. _____

2. _____

3. _____

I am grateful for this food:

I felt...

○ _____   ○ Content   ○ Sad

○ _____   ○ Inspired   ○ Anxious

○ Serene   ○ Cheerful   ○ Overwhelmed

○ Happy   ○ Hilarious   ○ Annoyed

○ Loving   ○ Balanced   ○ Disappointed

○ Kind   ○ Stressed   ○ Angry

Memory, thought or doodle of the day:

THOUGHT OF THE WEEK

"All grown-ups were once children...
but only few of them remember it."
- Antoine de Saint-Exupéry

Write about a great advice you've received.

Date: _____ **M T W T F S S**

I'm thankful for...

1. _____

2. _____

3. _____

Today this person was kind to me:

I felt...

- ○ _____
- ○ _____
- ○ Serene
- ○ Happy
- ○ Loving
- ○ Kind

- ○ Content
- ○ Inspired
- ○ Cheerful
- ○ Hilarious
- ○ Balanced
- ○ Stressed

- ○ Sad
- ○ Anxious
- ○ Overwhelmed
- ○ Annoyed
- ○ Disappointed
- ○ Angry

Memory, thought or doodle of the day:

Date: _____   **M T W T F S S**

I'm thankful for...

1. _____

2. _____

3. _____

Today I saw this act of kindness:

I felt...

- ○ _____
- ○ _____
- ○ Serene
- ○ Happy
- ○ Loving
- ○ Kind

- ○ Content
- ○ Inspired
- ○ Cheerful
- ○ Hilarious
- ○ Balanced
- ○ Stressed

- ○ Sad
- ○ Anxious
- ○ Overwhelmed
- ○ Annoyed
- ○ Disappointed
- ○ Angry

Memory, thought or doodle of the day:

Date: _____ **M T W T F S S**

I'm thankful for...

1. _____

2. _____

3. _____

Today I learned...

I felt...

○ _____   ○ Content   ○ Sad

○ _____   ○ Inspired   ○ Anxious

○ Serene   ○ Cheerful   ○ Overwhelmed

○ Happy   ○ Hilarious   ○ Annoyed

○ Loving   ○ Balanced   ○ Disappointed

○ Kind   ○ Stressed   ○ Angry

Memory, thought or doodle of the day:

Date: _____   **M T W T F S S**

I'm thankful for...

1. _____

2. _____

3. _____

Today I smiled because...

I felt...

○ _____   ○ Content   ○ Sad

○ _____   ○ Inspired   ○ Anxious

○ Serene   ○ Cheerful   ○ Overwhelmed

○ Happy   ○ Hilarious   ○ Annoyed

○ Loving   ○ Balanced   ○ Disappointed

○ Kind   ○ Stressed   ○ Angry

Memory, thought or doodle of the day:

Date: _____   **M T W T F S S**

I'm thankful for...

1. _____

2. _____

3. _____

I am grateful for this person:

I felt...

○ _____   ○ Content   ○ Sad

○ _____   ○ Inspired   ○ Anxious

○ Serene   ○ Cheerful   ○ Overwhelmed

○ Happy   ○ Hilarious   ○ Annoyed

○ Loving   ○ Balanced   ○ Disappointed

○ Kind   ○ Stressed   ○ Angry

Memory, thought or doodle of the day:

Date: _____   **M T W T F S S**

I'm thankful for...

1. _____

2. _____

3. _____

Things I did well today:

I felt...

- ○ _____
- ○ _____
- ○ Serene
- ○ Happy
- ○ Loving
- ○ Kind

- ○ Content
- ○ Inspired
- ○ Cheerful
- ○ Hilarious
- ○ Balanced
- ○ Stressed

- ○ Sad
- ○ Anxious
- ○ Overwhelmed
- ○ Annoyed
- ○ Disappointed
- ○ Angry

Memory, thought or doodle of the day:

Date: _____   **M T W T F S S**

I'm thankful for...

1. _____

2. _____

3. _____

┌───┐
│ I am grateful for this food: │
│   │
└───┘

I felt...

○ _____   ○ Content   ○ Sad
○ _____   ○ Inspired   ○ Anxious
○ Serene   ○ Cheerful   ○ Overwhelmed
○ Happy   ○ Hilarious   ○ Annoyed
○ Loving   ○ Balanced   ○ Disappointed
○ Kind   ○ Stressed   ○ Angry

┌───┐
│ Memory, thought or doodle of the day: │
│   │
│   │
│   │
│   │
│   │
│   │
│   │
│   │
│   │
│   │
└───┘

THOUGHT OF THE WEEK

"What makes the desert beautiful is that somewhere it hides a well."
- Antoine de Saint-Exupéry

The world is a good place because...

Date: _____   **M T W T F S S**

I'm thankful for...

1._____

2._____

3._____

Today this person was kind to me:

I felt...

○ _____   ○ Content   ○ Sad
○ _____   ○ Inspired   ○ Anxious
○ Serene   ○ Cheerful   ○ Overwhelmed
○ Happy   ○ Hilarious   ○ Annoyed
○ Loving   ○ Balanced   ○ Disappointed
○ Kind   ○ Stressed   ○ Angry

Memory, thought or doodle of the day:

Date: _____ **M T W T F S S**

I'm thankful for...

1. _____

2. _____

3. _____

Today I saw this act of kindness:

I felt...

- ○ _____
- ○ _____
- ○ Serene
- ○ Happy
- ○ Loving
- ○ Kind

- ○ Content
- ○ Inspired
- ○ Cheerful
- ○ Hilarious
- ○ Balanced
- ○ Stressed

- ○ Sad
- ○ Anxious
- ○ Overwhelmed
- ○ Annoyed
- ○ Disappointed
- ○ Angry

Memory, thought or doodle of the day:

Date: _____   **M T W T F S S**

I'm thankful for...

1. _____

2. _____

3. _____

Today I learned...

I felt...

- ○ _____
- ○ _____
- ○ Serene
- ○ Happy
- ○ Loving
- ○ Kind

- ○ Content
- ○ Inspired
- ○ Cheerful
- ○ Hilarious
- ○ Balanced
- ○ Stressed

- ○ Sad
- ○ Anxious
- ○ Overwhelmed
- ○ Annoyed
- ○ Disappointed
- ○ Angry

Memory, thought or doodle of the day:

Date: _____ **M T W T F S S**

I'm thankful for...

1. _____

2. _____

3. _____

Today I smiled because...

I felt...

○ _____ ○ Content ○ Sad

○ _____ ○ Inspired ○ Anxious

○ Serene ○ Cheerful ○ Overwhelmed

○ Happy ○ Hilarious ○ Annoyed

○ Loving ○ Balanced ○ Disappointed

○ Kind ○ Stressed ○ Angry

Memory, thought or doodle of the day:

Date: _____   **M T W T F S S**

I'm thankful for...

1. _____

2. _____

3. _____

┌───┐
│ I am grateful for this person: │
│   │
└───┘

I felt...

○ _____   ○ Content   ○ Sad
○ _____   ○ Inspired   ○ Anxious
○ Serene   ○ Cheerful   ○ Overwhelmed
○ Happy   ○ Hilarious   ○ Annoyed
○ Loving   ○ Balanced   ○ Disappointed
○ Kind   ○ Stressed   ○ Angry

┌───┐
│ Memory, thought or doodle of the day: │
│   │
│   │
│   │
│   │
│   │
│   │
│   │
│   │
│   │
│   │
└───┘

Date: _____   **M T W T F S S**

I'm thankful for...

1. _____

2. _____

3. _____

Things I did well today:

I felt...

○ _____	○ Content	○ Sad
○ _____	○ Inspired	○ Anxious
○ Serene	○ Cheerful	○ Overwhelmed
○ Happy	○ Hilarious	○ Annoyed
○ Loving	○ Balanced	○ Disappointed
○ Kind	○ Stressed	○ Angry

Memory, thought or doodle of the day:

Date: _____ **M T W T F S S**

I'm thankful for...

1. _____

2. _____

3. _____

┌───┐
│ I am grateful for this food: │
│   │
└───┘

I felt...

- ○ _____
- ○ _____
- ○ Serene
- ○ Happy
- ○ Loving
- ○ Kind

- ○ Content
- ○ Inspired
- ○ Cheerful
- ○ Hilarious
- ○ Balanced
- ○ Stressed

- ○ Sad
- ○ Anxious
- ○ Overwhelmed
- ○ Annoyed
- ○ Disappointed
- ○ Angry

┌───┐
│ Memory, thought or doodle of the day: │
│   │
│   │
│   │
│   │
│   │
│   │
│   │
│   │
└───┘

THOUGHT OF THE WEEK

"Every now and then it's good to stop climbing and appreciate the view from right where you are."
- Lori Deschene

What is one special talent you have and how do you use it?

....

....

....

....

....

....

....

....

Date: _____ **M T W T F S S**

I'm thankful for...

1. _____

2. _____

3. _____

Today this person was kind to me:

I felt...

○ _____ ○ Content ○ Sad

○ _____ ○ Inspired ○ Anxious

○ Serene ○ Cheerful ○ Overwhelmed

○ Happy ○ Hilarious ○ Annoyed

○ Loving ○ Balanced ○ Disappointed

○ Kind ○ Stressed ○ Angry

Memory, thought or doodle of the day:

Date: _____   **M T W T F S S**

I'm thankful for...

1. _____

2. _____

3. _____

Today I saw this act of kindness:

I felt...

○ _____   ○ Content   ○ Sad
○ _____   ○ Inspired   ○ Anxious
○ Serene   ○ Cheerful   ○ Overwhelmed
○ Happy   ○ Hilarious   ○ Annoyed
○ Loving   ○ Balanced   ○ Disappointed
○ Kind   ○ Stressed   ○ Angry

Memory, thought or doodle of the day:

Date: _____ **M T W T F S S**

I'm thankful for...

1. _____

2. _____

3. _____

Today I learned...

I felt...

○ _____   ○ Content   ○ Sad
○ _____   ○ Inspired   ○ Anxious
○ Serene   ○ Cheerful   ○ Overwhelmed
○ Happy   ○ Hilarious ○ Annoyed
○ Loving   ○ Balanced   ○ Disappointed
○ Kind   ○ Stressed   ○ Angry

Memory, thought or doodle of the day:

Date: _____   **M T W T F S S**

I'm thankful for...

1. _____

2. _____

3. _____

Today I smiled because...

I felt...

○ _____   ○ Content   ○ Sad

○ _____   ○ Inspired   ○ Anxious

○ Serene   ○ Cheerful   ○ Overwhelmed

○ Happy   ○ Hilarious   ○ Annoyed

○ Loving   ○ Balanced   ○ Disappointed

○ Kind   ○ Stressed   ○ Angry

Memory, thought or doodle of the day:

Date: _____   **M T W T F S S**

I'm thankful for...

1. _____

2. _____

3. _____

I am grateful for this person:

I felt...

- ○ _____
- ○ _____
- ○ Serene
- ○ Happy
- ○ Loving
- ○ Kind

- ○ Content
- ○ Inspired
- ○ Cheerful
- ○ Hilarious
- ○ Balanced
- ○ Stressed

- ○ Sad
- ○ Anxious
- ○ Overwhelmed
- ○ Annoyed
- ○ Disappointed
- ○ Angry

Memory, thought or doodle of the day:

Date: _____ **M T W T F S S**

I'm thankful for...

1. _____

2. _____

3. _____

Things I did well today:

I felt...
- ○ _____
- ○ _____
- ○ Serene
- ○ Happy
- ○ Loving
- ○ Kind

- ○ Content
- ○ Inspired
- ○ Cheerful
- ○ Hilarious
- ○ Balanced
- ○ Stressed

- ○ Sad
- ○ Anxious
- ○ Overwhelmed
- ○ Annoyed
- ○ Disappointed
- ○ Angry

Memory, thought or doodle of the day:

Date: _____   **M T W T F S S**

I'm thankful for...

1._____

2._____

3._____

┌──┐
│ I am grateful for this food: │
│   │
└──┘

I felt...

○ _____   ○ Content   ○ Sad
○ _____   ○ Inspired   ○ Anxious
○ Serene   ○ Cheerful   ○ Overwhelmed
○ Happy   ○ Hilarious   ○ Annoyed
○ Loving   ○ Balanced   ○ Disappointed
○ Kind   ○ Stressed   ○ Angry

┌──┐
│ Memory, thought or doodle of the day: │
│   │
│   │
│   │
│   │
│   │
│   │
│   │
│   │
│   │
└──┘

THOUGHT OF THE WEEK

"Gratitude makes sense of our past, brings peace for today, and creates a vision for tomorrow."
- Melody Beattie

Write about one of your happy memories.

Date: _____ **M T W T F S S**

I'm thankful for...

1. _____

2. _____

3. _____

Today this person was kind to me:

I felt...

○ _____ ○ Content   ○ Sad
○ _____ ○ Inspired   ○ Anxious
○ Serene   ○ Cheerful   ○ Overwhelmed
○ Happy   ○ Hilarious   ○ Annoyed
○ Loving   ○ Balanced   ○ Disappointed
○ Kind   ○ Stressed   ○ Angry

Memory, thought or doodle of the day:

Date: _____ **M T W T F S S**

I'm thankful for...

1. _____

2. _____

3. _____

> Today I saw this act of kindness:

I felt...

○ _____ ○ Content ○ Sad
○ _____ ○ Inspired ○ Anxious
○ Serene ○ Cheerful ○ Overwhelmed
○ Happy ○ Hilarious ○ Annoyed
○ Loving ○ Balanced ○ Disappointed
○ Kind ○ Stressed ○ Angry

> Memory, thought or doodle of the day:

Date: _____ **M T W T F S S**

I'm thankful for...

1. _____

2. _____

3. _____

Today I learned...

I felt...

○ _____ ○ Content ○ Sad

○ _____ ○ Inspired ○ Anxious

○ Serene ○ Cheerful ○ Overwhelmed

○ Happy ○ Hilarious ○ Annoyed

○ Loving ○ Balanced ○ Disappointed

○ Kind ○ Stressed ○ Angry

Memory, thought or doodle of the day:

Date: _____   **M T W T F S S**

I'm thankful for...

1. _____

2. _____

3. _____

Today I smiled because...

I felt...

○ _____	○ Content	○ Sad
○ _____	○ Inspired	○ Anxious
○ Serene	○ Cheerful	○ Overwhelmed
○ Happy	○ Hilarious	○ Annoyed
○ Loving	○ Balanced	○ Disappointed
○ Kind	○ Stressed	○ Angry

Memory, thought or doodle of the day:

Date: _____ **M T W T F S S**

I'm thankful for...

1. _____

2. _____

3. _____

I am grateful for this person:

I felt...

○ _____   ○ Content   ○ Sad
○ _____   ○ Inspired   ○ Anxious
○ Serene   ○ Cheerful   ○ Overwhelmed
○ Happy   ○ Hilarious   ○ Annoyed
○ Loving   ○ Balanced   ○ Disappointed
○ Kind   ○ Stressed   ○ Angry

Memory, thought or doodle of the day:

Date: _____   **M T W T F S S**

I'm thankful for...

1. _____

2. _____

3. _____

Things I did well today:

I felt...

○ _____   ○ Content   ○ Sad
○ _____   ○ Inspired   ○ Anxious
○ Serene   ○ Cheerful   ○ Overwhelmed
○ Happy   ○ Hilarious   ○ Annoyed
○ Loving   ○ Balanced   ○ Disappointed
○ Kind   ○ Stressed   ○ Angry

Memory, thought or doodle of the day:

Date: _____ **M T W T F S S**

I'm thankful for...

1. _____

2. _____

3. _____

I am grateful for this food:

I felt...

- ○ _____
- ○ _____
- ○ Serene
- ○ Happy
- ○ Loving
- ○ Kind

- ○ Content
- ○ Inspired
- ○ Cheerful
- ○ Hilarious
- ○ Balanced
- ○ Stressed

- ○ Sad
- ○ Anxious
- ○ Overwhelmed
- ○ Annoyed
- ○ Disappointed
- ○ Angry

Memory, thought or doodle of the day:

THOUGHT OF THE WEEK

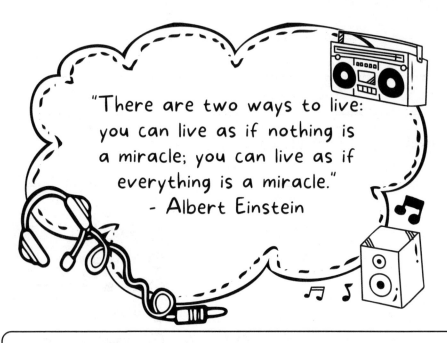

"There are two ways to live:
you can live as if nothing is
a miracle; you can live as if
everything is a miracle."
- Albert Einstein

What do you like about this season of the year?

Date: _____ **M T W T F S S**

I'm thankful for...

1. _____

2. _____

3. _____

Today this person was kind to me:

I felt...

○ _____ ○ Content ○ Sad
○ _____ ○ Inspired ○ Anxious
○ Serene ○ Cheerful ○ Overwhelmed
○ Happy ○ Hilarious ○ Annoyed
○ Loving ○ Balanced ○ Disappointed
○ Kind ○ Stressed ○ Angry

Memory, thought or doodle of the day:

Date: _____ **M T W T F S S**

I'm thankful for...

1. _____

2. _____

3. _____

Today I saw this act of kindness:

I felt...

○ _____   ○ Content   ○ Sad
○ _____   ○ Inspired   ○ Anxious
○ Serene   ○ Cheerful   ○ Overwhelmed
○ Happy   ○ Hilarious   ○ Annoyed
○ Loving   ○ Balanced   ○ Disappointed
○ Kind   ○ Stressed   ○ Angry

Memory, thought or doodle of the day:

Date: _____   **M T W T F S S**

I'm thankful for...

1. _____

2. _____

3. _____

Today I learned...

I felt...

○ _____ ○ Content   ○ Sad
○ _____ ○ Inspired ○ Anxious
○ Serene   ○ Cheerful ○ Overwhelmed
○ Happy   ○ Hilarious ○ Annoyed
○ Loving   ○ Balanced ○ Disappointed
○ Kind   ○ Stressed ○ Angry

Memory, thought or doodle of the day:

Date: _____   **M T W T F S S**

I'm thankful for...

1. _____

2. _____

3. _____

Today I smiled because...

I felt...

○ _____   ○ Content   ○ Sad
○ _____   ○ Inspired   ○ Anxious
○ Serene   ○ Cheerful   ○ Overwhelmed
○ Happy   ○ Hilarious   ○ Annoyed
○ Loving   ○ Balanced   ○ Disappointed
○ Kind   ○ Stressed   ○ Angry

Memory, thought or doodle of the day:

Date: _____   **M T W T F S S**

I'm thankful for...

1. _____

2. _____

3. _____

I am grateful for this person:

I felt...

- ○ _____
- ○ _____
- ○ Serene
- ○ Happy
- ○ Loving
- ○ Kind

- ○ Content
- ○ Inspired
- ○ Cheerful
- ○ Hilarious
- ○ Balanced
- ○ Stressed

- ○ Sad
- ○ Anxious
- ○ Overwhelmed
- ○ Annoyed
- ○ Disappointed
- ○ Angry

Memory, thought or doodle of the day:

Date: _____   **M T W T F S S**

I'm thankful for...

1. _____

2. _____

3. _____

Things I did well today:

I felt...

- ○ _____
- ○ _____
- ○ Serene
- ○ Happy
- ○ Loving
- ○ Kind

- ○ Content
- ○ Inspired
- ○ Cheerful
- ○ Hilarious
- ○ Balanced
- ○ Stressed

- ○ Sad
- ○ Anxious
- ○ Overwhelmed
- ○ Annoyed
- ○ Disappointed
- ○ Angry

Memory, thought or doodle of the day:

Date: _____   **M T W T F S S**

I'm thankful for...

1. _____

2. _____

3. _____

I am grateful for this food:

I felt...

○ _____   ○ Content   ○ Sad
○ _____   ○ Inspired   ○ Anxious
○ Serene   ○ Cheerful   ○ Overwhelmed
○ Happy   ○ Hilarious   ○ Annoyed
○ Loving   ○ Balanced   ○ Disappointed
○ Kind   ○ Stressed   ○ Angry

Memory, thought or doodle of the day:

THOUGHT OF THE WEEK

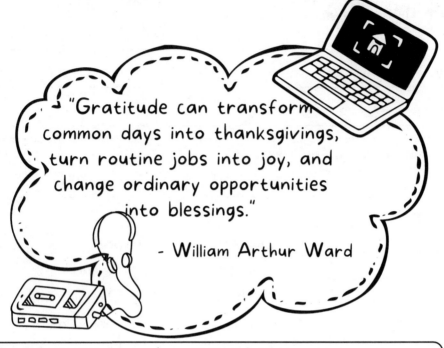

"Gratitude can transform common days into thanksgivings, turn routine jobs into joy, and change ordinary opportunities into blessings."

- William Arthur Ward

Look around the room. It is filled with little and big wonders. Write about the things you see that you're grateful for.

....

....

....

....

....

....

....

....

....

Date: _____   **M T W T F S S**

I'm thankful for...

1. _____

2. _____

3. _____

Today this person was kind to me:

I felt...

- ◯ _____
- ◯ _____
- ◯ Serene
- ◯ Happy
- ◯ Loving
- ◯ Kind

- ◯ Content
- ◯ Inspired
- ◯ Cheerful
- ◯ Hilarious
- ◯ Balanced
- ◯ Stressed

- ◯ Sad
- ◯ Anxious
- ◯ Overwhelmed
- ◯ Annoyed
- ◯ Disappointed
- ◯ Angry

Memory, thought or doodle of the day:

Date: _____   **M T W T F S S**

I'm thankful for...

1. _____

2. _____

3. _____

Today I saw this act of kindness:

I felt...

O _____   O Content   O Sad
O _____   O Inspired   O Anxious
O Serene   O Cheerful   O Overwhelmed
O Happy   O Hilarious   O Annoyed
O Loving   O Balanced   O Disappointed
O Kind   O Stressed   O Angry

Memory, thought or doodle of the day:

Date: _____ **M T W T F S S**

I'm thankful for...

1. _____

2. _____

3. _____

Today I learned...

I felt...

○ _____ ○ Content ○ Sad

○ _____ ○ Inspired ○ Anxious

○ Serene ○ Cheerful ○ Overwhelmed

○ Happy ○ Hilarious ○ Annoyed

○ Loving ○ Balanced ○ Disappointed

○ Kind ○ Stressed ○ Angry

Memory, thought or doodle of the day:

Date: _____   **M T W T F S S**

I'm thankful for...

1. _____

2. _____

3. _____

Today I smiled because...

I felt...

○ _____   ○ Content   ○ Sad
○ _____   ○ Inspired   ○ Anxious
○ Serene   ○ Cheerful   ○ Overwhelmed
○ Happy   ○ Hilarious ○ Annoyed
○ Loving   ○ Balanced   ○ Disappointed
○ Kind   ○ Stressed   ○ Angry

Memory, thought or doodle of the day:

Date: _____   **M T W T F S S**

I'm thankful for...

1. _____

2. _____

3. _____

I am grateful for this person:

I felt...

- ○ _____
- ○ _____
- ○ Serene
- ○ Happy
- ○ Loving
- ○ Kind

- ○ Content
- ○ Inspired
- ○ Cheerful
- ○ Hilarious
- ○ Balanced
- ○ Stressed

- ○ Sad
- ○ Anxious
- ○ Overwhelmed
- ○ Annoyed
- ○ Disappointed
- ○ Angry

Memory, thought or doodle of the day:

Date: _____ **M T W T F S S**

I'm thankful for...

1. _____

2. _____

3. _____

Things I did well today:

I felt...

- ○ _____
- ○ _____
- ○ Serene
- ○ Happy
- ○ Loving
- ○ Kind

- ○ Content
- ○ Inspired
- ○ Cheerful
- ○ Hilarious
- ○ Balanced
- ○ Stressed

- ○ Sad
- ○ Anxious
- ○ Overwhelmed
- ○ Annoyed
- ○ Disappointed
- ○ Angry

Memory, thought or doodle of the day:

Date: _____   **M T W T F S S**

I'm thankful for...

1. _____

2. _____

3. _____

I am grateful for this food:

I felt...

○ _____   ○ Content   ○ Sad

○ _____   ○ Inspired   ○ Anxious

○ Serene   ○ Cheerful   ○ Overwhelmed

○ Happy   ○ Hilarious   ○ Annoyed

○ Loving   ○ Balanced   ○ Disappointed

○ Kind   ○ Stressed   ○ Angry

Memory, thought or doodle of the day:

THOUGHT OF THE WEEK

"You're never alone when
you're reading a book."
- Susan Wiggs

Which book are you grateful for? Why do you like this book?

Date: _____ **M T W T F S S**

I'm thankful for...

1. _____

2. _____

3. _____

Today this person was kind to me:

I felt...

○ _____   ○ Content   ○ Sad
○ _____   ○ Inspired   ○ Anxious
○ Serene   ○ Cheerful   ○ Overwhelmed
○ Happy   ○ Hilarious   ○ Annoyed
○ Loving   ○ Balanced   ○ Disappointed
○ Kind   ○ Stressed   ○ Angry

Memory, thought or doodle of the day:

Date: _____ **M T W T F S S**

I'm thankful for...

1. _____

2. _____

3. _____

Today I saw this act of kindness:

I felt...

○ _____ ○ Content ○ Sad

○ _____ ○ Inspired ○ Anxious

○ Serene ○ Cheerful ○ Overwhelmed

○ Happy ○ Hilarious ○ Annoyed

○ Loving ○ Balanced ○ Disappointed

○ Kind ○ Stressed ○ Angry

Memory, thought or doodle of the day:

Date: _____   **M T W T F S S**

I'm thankful for...

1. _____

2. _____

3. _____

Today I learned...

I felt...

○ _____   ○ Content   ○ Sad

○ _____   ○ Inspired   ○ Anxious

○ Serene   ○ Cheerful   ○ Overwhelmed

○ Happy   ○ Hilarious   ○ Annoyed

○ Loving   ○ Balanced   ○ Disappointed

○ Kind   ○ Stressed   ○ Angry

Memory, thought or doodle of the day:

Date: _____   **M T W T F S S**

I'm thankful for...

1. _____

2. _____

3. _____

Today I smiled because...

I felt...

○ _____   ○ Content   ○ Sad
○ _____   ○ Inspired   ○ Anxious
○ Serene   ○ Cheerful   ○ Overwhelmed
○ Happy   ○ Hilarious   ○ Annoyed
○ Loving   ○ Balanced   ○ Disappointed
○ Kind   ○ Stressed   ○ Angry

Memory, thought or doodle of the day:

Date: _____ **M T W T F S S**

I'm thankful for...

1. _____

2. _____

3. _____

I am grateful for this person:

I felt...

- ○ _____
- ○ _____
- ○ Serene
- ○ Happy
- ○ Loving
- ○ Kind

- ○ Content
- ○ Inspired
- ○ Cheerful
- ○ Hilarious
- ○ Balanced
- ○ Stressed

- ○ Sad
- ○ Anxious
- ○ Overwhelmed
- ○ Annoyed
- ○ Disappointed
- ○ Angry

Memory, thought or doodle of the day:

Date: _____ **M T W T F S S**

I'm thankful for...

1. _____

2. _____

3. _____

Things I did well today:

I felt...

- ○ _____
- ○ _____
- ○ Serene
- ○ Happy
- ○ Loving
- ○ Kind

- ○ Content
- ○ Inspired
- ○ Cheerful
- ○ Hilarious
- ○ Balanced
- ○ Stressed

- ○ Sad
- ○ Anxious
- ○ Overwhelmed
- ○ Annoyed
- ○ Disappointed
- ○ Angry

Memory, thought or doodle of the day:

Date: _____   **M T W T F S S**

I'm thankful for...

1. _____

2. _____

3. _____

I am grateful for this food:

I felt...

- ○ _____
- ○ _____
- ○ Serene
- ○ Happy
- ○ Loving
- ○ Kind

- ○ Content
- ○ Inspired
- ○ Cheerful
- ○ Hilarious
- ○ Balanced
- ○ Stressed

- ○ Sad
- ○ Anxious
- ○ Overwhelmed
- ○ Annoyed
- ○ Disappointed
- ○ Angry

Memory, thought or doodle of the day:

Coloring Books by Julia Rivers

COLORING BOOK

Serene Little Village

The Wondrous Life Behind the Garden Walls

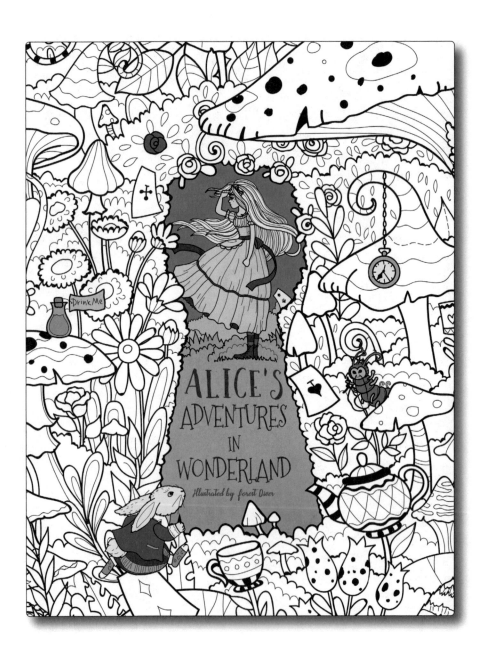

Coloring Books by Julia Rivers

Website: www.JuliaRivers.com
Facebook: www.JuliaRivers.com/facebook

Made in the USA
Thornton, CO
11/06/23 14:33:44

2c7c2495-f20e-4b4b-bc75-0b69a4c64a38R01